The Reservoir

The
Reservoir

Poems by Donna Stonecipher

The University of Georgia Press

Athens and London

Published by the University of Georgia Press

Athens, Georgia 30602

© 2002 by Donna Stonecipher

All rights reserved

Designed by April Leidig-Higgins

Set in Monotype Garamond by Copperline Book Services

Printed and bound by Thomson-Shore, Inc.

The paper in this book meets the guidelines for
permanence and durability of the Committee on
Production Guidelines for Book Longevity of the
Council on Library Resources.

Printed in the United States of America

06 05 04 03 02   P   5 4 3 2 1

Library of Congress Cataloging-in-Publication Data

Stonecipher, Donna, 1969–

The reservoir: poems / by Donna Stonecipher.

p. cm. — (The contemporary poetry series)

ISBN 0-8203-2463-9 (pbk. : alk. paper)

I. Title. II. Contemporary poetry series (University of Georgia Press)

PS3619.T685 R47 2002

811'.6 — dc21   2002006737

British Library Cataloging-in-Publication Data available

For my parents

and for Alex and Sarah

"Exquisite hours, enveloped in light and silence,
  to have known them once is to have always
  a terrible standard of enjoyment"— Henry James

"A beauty not explicable, is dearer than a beauty which
  we can see to the end of"— Ralph Waldo Emerson

CONTENTS

Grateful acknowledgment is made to the editors of the following journals, in which some of these poems originally appeared: *Denver Quarterly, Field, Indiana Review, New American Writing, Terra Incognita,* and *Web Conjunctions.*

Thank you to my family and friends, who are inextricable from these poems; to Sasha; to Lise and Cole, for valuable guidance; and to Pep, for the spur.

.

The Reservoir

Album

Anything seen through an arch is instantly picturesque. Why keep hoping things will speak for themselves, without your aid? The small wish for a tableau. The sunset might well bear you off on its pulleys of delight, the buildings are still strewn vacantly around the square. But you know what to frame. You know how to count. Arch flowing into arch flowing into arch, and through the last arch, what was dumb will speak. After all, it is the halos that tell us who the saints are. Rows of poplars: somewhere, a river, and workers bathing. Won't it all be laid out for you in sequence in the end, what has truly fallen into your frame? And everything else, the ungroomed land, the dead tea-roses, the body moving out of the shot. Who wouldn't be sentimental, given half the chance.

White Mouth

I had forgotten all about the star inside the apple, eating my way
through orchardsful in the intervening years, years marked by

Who does not judge each heart by halving it from the top instead
of scoring delicately around the girth? Still,

If I could fill myself with milk I'd be the old statue weathering in
the yard: evangelical, cicatrixed with white roses, the white of

My heart is as sad and wide as the side of a barn, the town drunk
said. Anyone can hit it, and quite frequently

But forgiveness is not in the purist's white apothecary. Skin secretes,
a mouth like oil never dries, and desire does not stay inside the lines

The face of the statue in the wild yard is soft and smeared as though
definition itself were an affront — herein nature's woozy story,

How "human" is human enough. Little rescues are at hand, angels in
plainclothes, but how can we know inside whom embark the seeds of our

As I stood holding my face up to the night sky the stars in their
pristine arrangements pricked every last swollen thing inside me, as if

For the larger the target of your heart, the more you must smelt yourself down to the slick business of forgiving

Forgiveness the liquid eating away at the cool white stars of the sugar. Intransigence the cream billowing up through the dark

I hold with white hands the purity of my own arrangement, while the brown star glows forgotten inside the pristine cage of each

In the tribunal of the streets I judge and condemn, never by choice but because we do what comes naturally

Show me, the town drunk said, one star in the night sky that is not waiting to be eaten by the spacious white mouth of the sun

(1)

Everyone's obsessed with their own story. I was thinking about how her beautiful singing voice sits useless in her body like a folded bird as she goes about her day, arranging the implements in her bag, tightening her shoestrap. (how much of a letter is a self-portrait) Some secrets bear occasional telling. Others build jealously like storms, and when a day dawns wet and cups its moistness, all kinds of lesions are possible. In the white sky, a lesion of violet.

(2)

The bee is more afraid of you than you of it, my father said. I am so tired of speaking, of the gears and levers to adjust and pedals asking for my feet and hands. If steam comes out my ears it is just the engine of the what-to-say overheating again. (to impress upon you the insignia of my distress) We are drawn to each other like sinners to cathedrals. Words come in many varieties of confession, but if you come too clean there is a danger of ending up empty.

(3)

Cleanliness polishes American bodies to the smoothness of products.
Not to be vulgar, but skin soaks up or reflects the wearer's "inner beauty"
the way that meadows tell too much about the weather — sometimes
spoiling our picnic. (please, do not meet me outside the confessional)
Ants stitch their black embroidery on the nectarines and the strawberries
and the French bread, they do not mind ruining our plans, our afternoon.

(4)

When the bee finally stung I was sipping in the blur of honeysuckle
vines at dusk. My parents were not at home. The only word for bee Mme.
Shakibniya knew was "mosquito" and she lay me down and gave me rock-
candy from the jar in her kitchen. (I am telling you the truth as I see it —
do I see it) My eye was fat the next day for school pictures. An American
photographer, he called me "Peaches." So for one night a mosquito con-
ferred a sting. Misunderstanding I'd say has a venom it doesn't know itself
to possess.

(5)

In conversation, some words are dead-ends and others aqueducts. The flow must be regulated. Keep some water for the reservoir. Never spend it. (the heart is many-storied) Loose-lipped, I sometimes poured secrets into whatever vessel. From vessel to vessel, a burden displaced. I was anxious to tell my version of the story of what the world has done to me — but you must be careful how many times you ask to be rescued.

(6)

Because confession is ruled by ecstasy and not forthrightness, which anyone can verify: the face rapt with the flowing forth of all that — houses swept downriver, walls separating from roofs — was held in place by gravity and the reliable open-and-shut of day. Of all that loves the body like disease. (of my passion, whom can I convince) The willing ear held aloft like a lantern in the dark garden guides the confessor forth, the confessor who has become a seeker of the one shining thing buried in a puzzle of dark leaves.

One's own story fascinates such that others are only echoes. Where an aspect mirrors an aspect, where something I want to do or be, you have done or are and then you reach me, you become part of my story. (the reservoir placid through the seasons, may save us) The cynic is speaking. She has seen the cycles of attraction and disillusion whirling through the charged expanse — thanks to sentences and their trestles, vaunting what in certain light appear to be bridges.

The Visit

In the end, the leaves don't fall very far at all. Incessant downward spirals, projected yellow voluptuaries — all soon land down on the lawn. Drawing the eye up — to the empty dark branch. A leaf is fleeting; a carpet of leaves lasts through spring. And the health of a tree is determined by the circumference of its trunk.

Or so said the evangelist gardener. As in, the trees that remain rooted longest will have more girth to show for their faith. Then Dutch elm disease arrives in America. Inside each tree is a secret diary. But it is unkind to blame the city planners, who gridded long rows of wood houses shaded by neatly spaced elms that were meant to be loyal.

I turn the page to a single arabesque of gold forgotten hair. The plantation had a highway built right through it. It is as if I have put a seashell to my ear when I am in the "Pink Room" — the master bedroom minus its master. He was nursed on the sleigh bed I am to sleep in surrounded by wallpaper of regularized roses.

In the book of quotations (for people who can't remember exactly who said exactly what) (it is a point of pride — to remember), quotations are arrayed like butterflies in a compendium for rapt identification. No shame in being starstruck. Everything in town is star-struck, including the keys laid on bureaus and the heads on large white pillows.

The fallen leaves lie on the grass in plain view of the tree they've fallen from. But the only eye to be seen is that of the starling, whose black feathers have winterized so that he appears papered over with a diagram of the night sky. Surely there must be farther to fall — surely the wish to keep falling, can be granted —

The plantation lost its grove of black walnuts, and we are invited to see where the grove once stood from the rooftop observatory. We climb and climb up staircases through roomfuls of old brown books. The last peacock drags its beautiful burden through the dirt, but only one small purple feather can be found on the lawn.

The aphorism has already grown a pair of baby wings: that is why we open the book with our nets ready. The inheritor lives in the smallest room in the house, away from the highboys and the portraits and the snuffboxes. Which he mentions he will not part with. He plots out a walk for us among the fields planted with tobacco and soy.

Slow methodical swirls of quince-colored leaves — the eye cannot acknowledge each leaf, as a city sky cannot allow in many stars. The city smokes like the brain, possessive. The collector dies with the catalogue in his head only, and so an order dies. And so the objects must be tallied over again, tallied and photographed and sold.

But it's the portraits I remember when I try to picture where it was I was. The dark girl in the blue satin dress whose face would admit no gazer, her shoulders bare and cold. Odd that I did not break a precious figurine. Odd that the peacock's club-foot kept it from the tree, which kept it from the owl, which is why it is the last peacock.

The Guest

The spider rests motionless among its needlepoint legs, out of the way of the sun. Who could sit so peacefully next to the clock gathering the hours in its nicked pastoral hands? Only a handful of girls grows to awareness of the dark silence exactly at the center of the wedding — the missing piece of the lace puzzle only separation will fit.

One evening we followed the tracks of the sugar-footed fly. The letter that said "There's something I've been meaning to tell you" or "Forgive me for what I am about to reveal" had not yet come. Square day after square day foretold that it would be peacetime, deep peacetime. The wood swelled, and the landlord struggled at night to close and lock his own door.

She apologized profusely, saying the bee must have been baked right into the cake. She let herself out the back and dragged a chair out under the moon, hoping for — a lume? When at last her shadow troubled the circumference of the porch-light, she said to us: *I think perfection is a needle, and I have smothered my life in stacks and stacks of hay.*

Only one cigarette was left — who would end up veiled behind the orientalist gestures of the smoker? The birds — no, this narrator could not say what kind — gravitated in a garland toward the tree, where they began eating according to a math — one cherry for each decompression of feathers, one grub for each glance down to the grass.

The record kept spinning as if to please the needle. So we all hoped for something private to excavate our own engraved refrains. The guest had been up in the guest room for hours, presumably weeping. I suppose what I really wanted that summer was a chandelier of now, but only nostalgia sparkled.

The photographic smile was the worst possible invention for the human mouth. Joy carved into rinds, it has a price. Like an infection the choice I had made stole into me — and briefly I was ignorant in bliss

As with certain stars, a direct gaze makes the truth disappear into the night's dark folds. By definition: Inamorata: (fem.) "the beloved"; Inamorato: (masc.) "the lover"; so one is the target, and one is the arrow

Perhaps the transgression lay in wanting two things equally, the way the moon — trapped in its succession of public rendings — long ago refused to unhand either light or dark

The cold truth is, I was not present at the scene of my decision. I was gazing into the mirror getting to know me. The blue of the crushed-up night outside encouraged both a truth-telling and a concealment

When I learned that each decision was freighted with irrevocable meaning, I tried to stop deciding. I would wait to be hailed. But my decisions thrived without me, filing quarterly reports, procuring funding

My mouth was an empty frame; in my heart lay the picture. The souvenir stands sold Victorian viewfinders through which twin photographs of naughty Parisiennes fused into one. I knew behind their dreamy dark eyes gleamed the evening's cherry tarts

Through a forest of black cameras the tourists roam, taking. He who wields the machine will own each arch of the colonnade, each gaping gap. But the gentle frown of the bridge laughs last when its likeness disappoints in little formats

In a restaurant once I heard a man say, in life there are the pimps and there are the prostitutes. Every hunter knows how the thing he covets most escapes just at the instant of possession

Yet, before there were smiles, there were eyes like thin patches on frozen ponds through which boys broke and drowned while the other children splintered into the icy woods — was such despair any nearer to the truth

The infection lost pity and took me. Did the transgression lie in wanting two things equally — the way certain stars seem to want to be both seen and hidden? — I took to my bed with purgative syrup

Indecision, it seemed, was pure arrogance; so was decision. Life took sly turns like the gathering of the weather, and in the antechamber of my fever I was moved to ask, who's holding the reins of this animal

His model I sank to my knees before the one who captured me. I had had enough of punishment; I had come for my reward. But when his photographs of me emerged from the darkroom — I, I was not in them —

Du côté de chez Swann

My grandfather was a barber, but he owned a full set of Proust. Do trees massed together consent to be called "forest" or is each tree chafing against the crowd — the 'I' voiced through the bird nestled reliably in its depths? In every bird's chest sits a little mechanism chuffing out songs. I know the whole repertoire, chapter and verse. In the evening, I know the bittersweet of letting another speak through you.

A l'ombre des jeunes filles en fleurs

Magnificent books not augured by his beginnings. Because my parents bought my sister a silver spoon in every country, I thought the word was "silvenir." When the man I am in love with finally writes me a letter I fling all the objects from my room so it can glow untainted, enshrined on a pale shelf, and I its tear-stained penitent. Oh for a house with a honey-comb of rooms in which to slip each bit of proof my life has meant something to someone. Even if that someone is only me.

Le côté de Guermantes

In other words, my grandfather wasn't born with a "deep" book in his mouth. How much nicer it is to romanticize someone you've never known — how nice it is to romanticize. To know too much is to feel the portrait-gallery transmogrify into the shooting-gallery. The moon has a side it never shows us, and the romance of that is what I am after. The way the two sides of a spoon show you right-side-up or upside down.

Sodome et Gomorrhe

No one else in the history of our family ever kept books. When the Music Hall was torn down to make room for a slim hotel, people came to buy a single finial, a bit of mirror, the escutcheon that framed a keyhole through which in the newer moon of this century a naive eye may have become wise. At Masada, we were each allowed to steal a small piece of rock. Even as we speak, deer are stepping gingerly as jewel-thieves among the dark masses of the trees.

La Prisonnière

The books left my grandmother's house with my grandfather. Photographs fetishize. In every country, we let the souvenir stands bedazzle us, my brother chose a mug. A boot-shaped mug of glass, of course, in Italy. If windows are truly frozen, there are looks I have given the night sky that would have melted the dormer. In every house there is at least one girl with eyes of fire. In place of her heart a small box, when opened, incites a mechanical melody and a ballerina pirouetting in a stiff net skirt.

Albertine Disparue

I never really knew my father, said my father. For he did something so deliciously bad he sweetened, sweetened the plot. And so a deer becomes venison. And so a grandfather becomes a romantic figure, a handsome barber with a set of magnificent books. Something we have too much or too little of, is culture. One house has rooms furred with books, while the house next door is smooth. Is culture in the blood? Is this thing between the moon and myself personal?

Le Temps retrouvé

Though the barber learned to speak in a shack with a floor of earth, this is the great blind eye of America, and by the day he died he had read the collected works of Marcel Proust. In every country, I received a doll. For example, a Spanish dancer with castanets and a plastic mantilla. This was decided by powers high above me. Each Saturday for three years my parents courted the carpet-sellers in the bazaars, weighing, fingering, planning for the grand acquisition.

At the garage sale, my parents and aunts and uncles took turns making pleasantries and change from the tackle box. The complete set of Proust fetched fifty cents. I was five. While I was packing in my little suitcase dolls from Egypt and Thailand, they were giving out "international" dolls at gas stations all across America. The Swiss miss if I recall was a smash hit. We left the country without any carpets. The dolls in their national costumes are straining their eyes through the dark of a cardboard morgue in my mother's basement, even as we speak.

(1)

Once upon a time secrets were cheap, easily bought and
easily spent, moving angelically through the agency

of the mouth, until the day a secret swept up to the lips
that could not be told, capsizing as it would

everything, and so the secret stayed inside, and rose in
value, until it sank and became

a lake, keeping its decorous hem, contained by a law
more persuasive than the laws

of spilling over, declining the caravansaray of the mouth,
where so many

little sojourners have undressed, under the spell of false
security, a mouth's worth

of daggers hidden throughout the silken stuff. It learned
its lessons from the mouths

of rivers, where the sea in its green answerlessness
staggers the river's arrow, so sure in its slim

intent, aiming,— aiming,— only to come apart at its
delicate seams in the mouth. The fulsomeness,

the unplumbable depths of the mouth. But the secret
kept its lake, a blue locket on the map,

consequences moldering along the bottom, held inside
that cloudy skull, and what dreamy swimmer

would disquiet such innocent vows: to decline
brackishness, to glow like a pale-blue opal

for itself and only itself, rim open-hearted enough to
allow a plot, but never —

to be broken. Voices porter within them unbidden
luggage for the next destination, and you too have a mouth

that greets the sea.

(2)

For what is a storm in the sky to the storm sounding
throughout the fragile bluebells of this trembling

settlement: the garden outside: sown with vows easily
abandoned when brides and grooms no longer

look at each other, the wind twisting through this ghost
town of moments forsaken, or moments

too, too much taken. The secret starts a storm inside the
mouth, and because the rain

is held inside — pale-blue clouds heavy with portent
reined in — the mouth

bespeaks a weight it never before possessed, and then
the body feels the secret sink

like a stone down the rosary of the river, because a secret
is riverine. A secret cannot be

lacustrine. A secret must have its season, but o may the
ruckus be interior, and the rain beflower the archival

garden inside, dim with feverfew and bog violets, which
in their seeds remember the lake, pale-blue opal

of aspic, where the voyage is always headed due north,
due south, minus

the black ribbon of a destination, and the voice of the
secret swept downriver speaks

of here and only here, and apotheosizes the lake, and
fights with all its clandestine force against

the aphrodisiac of the current.

The Needle's Eye

In the letter I want to write but won't I'd tell him this: It is easier for the camel to squeeze through the needle's eye than for the watchful to enter the beautiful kingdom. If I daydream about living in a convent for a time, it doesn't mean I don't fear the silence that renders everything black and white. In the courtyard a drill clatters; the mirrors inside the birds' chests reflect this dark noise until their own throats open. If he wanted me on my knees so I wanted him; and so we were doubly unleveraged. This is the city, there is nothing to take us out of ourselves. Things are surprisingly tolerable until I touch my own body: It knows my hand is not his, it wants to murder me for this.

The Scar

As if summer existed, in real materials, hot to the touch, like sand giving itself to sun. There was a host of water: I dove deeply. In the evening we set off down the lantern-lit streets in quest of erasure.

It was hot that night and as you stirred your coffee you informed me I had accidentally ordered a belly-dancer. Darling, I still hold my doomed vigil. We rushed unregaled back to the hotel, hushed by the sky's lordly authority.

In the end it was you who pointed out the sign: Šanzelizé: Belly-dancing. It took me longer to resist the hotel pool beckoning. Somehow we never did time love in the hotel room to the call of the muezzin.

But there was never a moment when I stood in the sand and said to myself: It is summer. Was it you keeping me seasonless, damselling me into that whitewashed room where the only rescue my love knew was your . . . distress?

Or, we could be walking down the real Champs Elysées in the height of summer. Someone was talking about a woman who, in any expanse, could always extract the four-leafed clover. But everywhere I looked I saw only sand.

If motion were the sovereign good, and destination, a daydream — we were in awe of the anchor, glinting. From the beach the waves looked like narrow white scars on the blue, hurrying to the port's little ablution.

I swam and swam, and when I had swum out far enough away from you — a dot on the shore — I realized I didn't care to be alone with that stranger. The captain struck up the boat. I left her out there in the waves to I cared not what fate.

From town to town, we heard rumors of belly-dancers, the existence of whom was not confirmed. I noticed a scar on me, whose provenance was unknown. We were climbing into a boat whose name had weathered away.

I was marked; I had a scar; the globe had not spared me. Each grain of sand was a tiny tombstone, but we were the living. The mosquitoes were brushing you where I had, erasing the fading traces of me, an infestation.

I gave myself one final, unmistakable shove. But she managed to straggle back to the shore and sat down, panting, on my towel, next to me. Suddenly dusk fell. Where were you? Reading a novel, behind one of the lit squares high up on the hill.

Don't you know, I said to myself, there will always be a map, aquamarine? And the speed-of-light escapism of names. Even if the spire gains speed as you chase it. Even if last night, the town's one true bellydancer was washed irretrievably out to sea.

The scar is a plain gravemarker, never letting the skin forget. In vain we look: the story that caused the scar has weathered away. But every grain of sand running through my hand had its grandeur once too — its grandeur roaming the sea.

If I swore the butterfly that day was vindictive, lurching again and again toward my face with a decipherable goal, liquid undaunted, because I'd forgotten the lilliputian caterpillar my fingers found earlier eating the leaves of the rosemary. It wore a small stroke of bright orange. This is addressed to you, lost wax.

O my god my feelers. And don't things begin exactly like this, exactly, in miniature? Yes, the tightly wrinkled buds of that flower *do* lead me to believe last year's done violet gusts were just stuffed back into their cases — and the year's before that, and the year's before that — a choker of years

The poppy waits in its hairy hood. The iris cracks out of its dead tutelary paper. How can this bud in my hand pretend it has come from the holy nowhere of the new? The snow has not gone far, it will return — and not long after, the horse-drawn sleigh with its quartet of ideal occupants, and faint-hearted bells

As a fortress, the skin is a failure. Down, down, down, the eyelids come, but in front of them the corps de ballet pirouettes and pirouettes on, multiplying its swans, and the first ballerina will not be riven down to one governable feather. If the gauze were not so sheer, if the day didn't aureole a darkness

All the parched throats were drawn on to the orangerie. Its frosted glass glowed in the dim, a promise of ice. I lay down on the grass at dawn to lose my mind among the slim green pilgrims upholding their votives of dew. The juice spurts where the tooth breaks into the skin. A wayward tangerine, staining my flowering hands

The Chase

Does the snake-charmer truly charm the snake, or is it the idea of
the snake that charms the charmer into configuring the flute, the lips, the
spell, in the first place? This notion of desire as reciprocal gives the lie

to such satires as unrequited love. Last night the birds did *not*
suspend their joyful bickering while the woman cried for help in
the park at 4 a.m. Row upon row of darkened windows, like sealed
mouths,

kept to themselves. The one window with a light on was a face wet
with innocence, the gift some of us wish to spend more hurriedly than
others, as though it were a miasma precluding pure vision, who can say

at precisely what moment the masks make the costume ball begin.
In the second grade I outran Reza Khan from one end of the green play-
ground to the other, watching the grass lilt up under my feet; I outran his
little lips

that wanted to kiss me, or some other girl, it was the chase that
mattered, in the historical moment, in the springtime, in a foreign country,
in the late 1970s. In the back seat of rented cars I was gluttonous

with my daydreams like American bubblegum, a whole pack to my-
self, using this or that girl I had seen in the airport, at the hotel pool, whose
sequined swimsuit and back-flip I wished were mine, and whose life

I then appropriated, as though it were me remote in sequins, clutched
tight as a fist in a back-flip, this was all long before sex, a glimmer in my
eye, ascended. For a time it was the rage to hold your arms so tight

around a girl you made her faint, the boys wanted it too, I saw the
stairs back home like a ghostly ladder to an unsought answer, then came
to under a circle of boys with my T-shirt pushed above my

tiny breasts. It happened in the hotel garden. My cupboards were
bare. Before we even knew what rape was we wanted to accuse our P.E.
teacher of it, that fascist, though in fact we had no idea

what that meant, either. I am one of these who has no use for knowledge until its impassable bulk blocks my path, for instance, why was Deedee Sadigh, a better runner than me, back there in a heap on the grass, being covered with kisses

by Reza Khan? Was that his name? I remember hers better, as I remember all the girls unruly like vetch and helleborine flowering in the plot of my girlhood, tyrannical virgin queens, while the boys are almost all

vague — pale shavings of bark. There were enough pistils and stamens then that we did not notice the trees. In fact my heart was broken by a girl, this was many years before a man said to me, in college,

half of desire is awareness of the other's desire, which made my nightly sessions at the mirror downright erotic. If anyone had told me I had need of sequined swimsuits, filched inventories, I would have said no, I was sovereign

of my own demesne. But why were satin pillows the scene of so many girls' nightly dreams of transgression? The rapist and the ravisher each held out hands stigmataed with sticky candy, and any good girl

knew to back away from both. In truth in class we read so many
books about rape and war and rape in war that at night I began to ban-
dage my own body, as though the wounds had opened their manifold

red mouths all over me. What, after all, was "repudiation of the mas-
culine" but a wish to remember the heroine? There was a familiar ring to
charming and spurning, running and running, a resurrected belief

that it was she who could not be caught who would be ever sought,
something I read in a book somewhere, how wearying it is to pick up the
receiver and dial when you know for certain

the dialee will answer. The logic in Daphne's feathery tree. When did
we learn that exaggerated rejection is a garden-marker for buried desire?
And still I let the phone ring, though I am home, I have been

found. But last night there was a woman crying for help in the park,
I went down to look but was too afraid to look deeper, to sacrifice my
looking at the black altar of the bushes, why is the line so fine between
ravishment

and horror, the mind of the woman couldn't tell you, it is in a faint, and why will my legs not run, as in the old dream, though he is in pursuit? And suddenly he blocks my path, he is impassable, and I sink into a heap

on the grass, where he whispers in my ear about his great-grandmother's village, at the end of the war, and how, when the Russians came to liberate this village, all the men were still away, and so the soldiers

raped the women, well I mean (he said), the women wanted it, when the soldiers came knocking, the women opened up their doors, they hitched up their skirts, the women — let the soldiers — in

A new conception: You, too, might be the kind of person who does not write back. You always kneeled first because the hard ground seemed to discipline you to it, with its acres of truth. You truly believed we should do unto others as we would have them do unto us. And then the problem worried itself to the bone: what you would have others do unto you is surrender. Suddenly you catch a glimpse of yourself in the crowd: wearing dark glasses. You want to follow yourself. You want to write to yourself and feel the slow mortification of yourself not writing back. The virtue of the skyscraper is that it knows not how towering a flower it is, in the formal garden. No one notices the knickknacks. Martyrdom moves only one face to tears.

The Sea-Porcupine

A body impacting water sounds the world over the same. Same-nesses congregate. I am looking for the telling detail, the one misstep among the crowd climbing into the low boat for the swim in the secluded cove. Later, at exactly the right time, appetites will light up in bellies like stars.

Even beachcombing burdens me with its astoundingly usual yield. If I am hoping all day for a shell without a flaw, what singularity dignifies my quest? Faintly in my passport it is stamped, that I am the missionary's reverse: I have disembarked announcing my wish not to transform, but to be transformed.

(When I step on a sea-porcupine in the dark shallows and later, find a tiny constellation of quills stuck in my skin, the hotel-owner sends up a needle, though she will make no appearance herself. I am secretly pleased to be taking home something harder to get than cherry brandy or lavender sachets)

Another swimmer dives into the sea: a small cross dangling in the liquid throat of the violet-blue. There is a line where the air meets the sea; it is inviolable. Those who know, know how not to cross. I went with my friend into the Blue Grotto, where first she and then I disappeared into the intermittently blue pool.

I've been here before. I recognized it on the boat over, when my shadow began to be unmistakable on the water's shivering surface. The seashells glow with vacancies. We prepare in our room to walk down to the harbor-town and drink what the locals drink. We'd bathe in the local drink, if the hotel allowed.

Magnet

A line of white flowers glows as the darkness of a particular dusk furs down the transparent ground that hovers between foreground and background, that will not confer the secret of its stance upon the gloaming

viewer, the bird-adorer. This darkness duly darkens a primer of violets, gaunt tiger lilies, and flickering ash-leaves, but cannot extinguish the lamps of the short white flowers, so that each flower is infused

with a darkness that magnifies its whiteness. Sitting opposite my friend at the bar, I almost asked him to narrate me for me: staircase after staircase, landing after landing — and finials. So my character might be lost like any other roaming through a mildly interested storyteller's lazy architectonics. (I wanted the night to obscure me like that, with such amplification. I wanted to see myself like that, through the gossiper's

telescope, myself the magnetic portrait in the little locket. *The portrait in the little locket will not speak.* The objects in the gossiper's telescope never get larger or smaller.) A staircase is a staircase

is a staircase. And the back yard, with its rows of white pickets and its rusted lilacs, the back yard with its buried goldfish? Lying down on the sloping lawn, I never stopped hoping for the legendary pitcher of lemonade and translucent tumblers balanced gently on an old metal lid. O it was just a detail from a story read probably in childhood, no it was a floating reminiscence from the pond of a day

distilled from the long liquid of childhood, oh it scattered itself like the ice-blue petals of the hydrangeas clutched in my hands at the long-ago neighborhood may day parade . . . I almost asked my friend. Sitting opposite

me at the bar.

The Forest

The sun stole in like a snow-leopard, the window was powerless to resist. The curtains drifted indifferently, outside there were girls saturated with light unwitting, fingertips milky blossoms unbidden (leaf fitting neatly into leaf fitting neatly into leaf)

(The End.)

But all of this was after the fact. On the slow drive, in the long afternoon, in the late, votive summer, we came across the cautionary tale. Field upon field of charred sunflowers — Black Madonnas — tending their losses. Heads bowed, faces written upon, ashes, ashes —

(The End.)

But I had laid a trail of crumbs to lead me home. And the deeper I plunged the more heavenly was the gingerbread's scent —

Sun, the landlord who could not resist their milkmaid charms (and who made the roses lose their minds) —. The land was sown with seeds. I think the seeds were glowing —. But in the end too many acres proved unwilling to give up a harvest

(The End.)

Such clearings came only later. For years the mind had wandered through the vicarage of the forest, that gabled, verboten place — the mind had unraveled through the concentric circles of trees, the forest's true center fingerable everywhere, spiraling into, out of, the pith

(The End.)

The black throats of the birds high in the treetops took on a bluish cast as I ran past, and I thought to myself how meaningful it all is! how bathed in beauty!

Night was a constancy of beginnings. And that is why it was a day-light life. So some hard law said: lights out, head down — day — off — night — on — off — (leaf fitting neatly into leaf fitting neatly into leaf)

(The End.)

The day was a frangible skin covering the disordered bones of the night. Night, the velvet interrogation —. (Was the night a *staged* end?) — (the meaning gleamed in the skull's smile)

(The End.)

And the faster I ran, the more heavenly was the gingerbread's scent, the more crumbs of myself I surrendered to get to that clearing

One comes to the end of the forest. But not before growing hopelessly lost in the mapless middle —. One's stunned by the end of the forest. But not before the slowly swinging lanterns of the mindless middle —. One longs for the end of the forest (one loves the dark deciduousness of the middle)

(The End.)

When the end comes, when I am down to my last recognizable piece

On the slow drive — in the guise of interest — in a land without hills suddenly there were hills — this car unknown, this driver ungloving, and the vehicle cresting the first hill upon hill upon hill —

with more precision I traced in my head the path I had taken in, the path I would take back out —

(The End.)

when the end comes, when like the tiny pieces of a puzzle methodically unsolved I am down to my last recognizable piece

In an existence hinging upon endings, days spent listening for those thuds of the gavel when blessed judgment could begin — it was the promise of an end that led the figure to the edge of the forest, to the foreshortened avenue of inquiry, to the tentative, inexorable valentine of the night

The more heavenly was the gingerbread's scent

I have a secret I keep even from this sweetest reaper of secrets

The more heavenly was the gingerbread's scent

A secret even in the season of the oven, each of my clasps undone but one —

The more heavenly was the gingerbread's scent

A secret I keep from the galaxy of birds chortling in the forest: *I know the path back out — I have laid a trail of crumbs to lead me home.*

Wave

Seaside, the sun proves that I am hollow. Down by the water the sandcastle is a small irritant in the wave's mouth. My white shirt flutters above me, blinding with sunlight; a white butterfly navigates the tufts. It is for reaffirmation of certain knowledge that a pilgrim seeks out an uncertain landscape. Why, tonight, did the sunset tell me something I already know, when there is so much unseen goldenrod yet to clasp?

As the wave inundates the moat innocently built to protect the sandcastle, the sun effaces my small band of preserver light, flooding my limbs with its one dictum of utter cleanliness. But I am safe: no torrent of moral sunlight will ever divagate down my bones. The sand only grumbles sweetly; it will give in to my hips' demands. When I am gone from the beach, it's the darkness that will embed my memory.

The dawn is still unprecedented — but who's awake to see the dawn? If I am awake to see the dawn it means I haven't understood the night. As soon as the people leave the beach, the sand-crabs tiptoe out to weigh down their absence. I watch the evening tarnish. But this reclamation of shifting ground is fraught, with caution. As, away in the awakening town, people emerge gingerly from their hotel rooms to consider the dimly lit restaurants.

Words drift free of their captors, and that is what keeps drawing me back to the source of this emancipation. To which I am a willing captive. Down by the water, the children are building a sandcastle, but their laughter is blown to the small dunes behind the umbrella rental. I am lying in the sand, I am full of myself. Green grape after green grape breaks in my mouth without a sound.

The waves the sea will ruffle loose — but it reclaims them, one by one, by means of its magnetism. It can't part with a single drop. The pilgrim gropes for the borders of the dazzling landscape. My body full of sunlight makes no mark. And now I am the vial I wanted to own. "Cotton has no memory," the proprietor said, his hand patting the mattress. But the woodwork warped to say it won't forget.

Sparrows

Why are there so many sparrows in the bushes when the eye lights up at an isolation of color, oriole or cardinal, grackle, when my eye invites the sky to replace its gray with an infusion of blue particles, when the bluebell tells me to consume its ladder of blue? In the window, there is a face, and in the face there is an eye, and that eye is a jeweller.

I watched the actress stop speaking when words began to arrive in her mind already written, trapped in ink the instant they fluttered into air. This was an actress in a movie, no actress I knew. She was pinned to the four corners of the screen. I wanted to tell you about it, but you couldn't remove from my mouth my favorite mask.

No chair was exactly right. She brought him gaunt flowers. Each blue in the painting in the museum was tethered like a blood relative to each other blue. The first locust broke the cold silence of the summer dusk, the tiers and tiers of darkness. Down the path the fireflies formed and dissolved little quotes of constellations.

(Why are there so many sparrows? I waited *all night* for the throatful of petals —) O starry hotel, booked with dead unending guests. The vanishing powder sifts through its old sieve. I wanted to set my next word apart in a velvet jewel-case, and deep in the hollow of the word would abide a tiny flawed me.

It is true, one day all the butterflies did have blank wings. The park was supposed to represent itself, of course, as I asked the goldfinch to represent itself, as I asked for no questionable bramble. The mirror in its gold-leaf frame, the vanity mirror, the mirror with the goldfinch caught in its heart — no I am not responsible.

But when the deer, delicate thing, began stamping its taut hoof at me in my own back yard, I went in for my shears to cut the black-eyed susans. Dusk always does that (when I apprehend the dusk). I am not down on my knees in the dirt planting bulbs. Which means in spring, I will not be obliterated by tulips.

The Specialists

You came and went through my head like a small storm. It was only later I questioned the teacup. Distemper among the clouds, the solvent possible. I had forgotten my umbrella, so that each raindrop fell on me separately, a bit broken from the old whole.

Thus began another dreamy rampage through the small town of my mind. There he is, windblown and silent on the porch, the only man I'll ever love — and a series of husks on the threshing floor — and storefront after storefront of approximation.

Violence flowers the puzzle; but when the puzzle is solved, it vanishes —. In the museum, I saw the specialists hunched over the useless identical fragments of Saint Francis. I saw the relief perched like light upon their brows. Is a fragment a true fragment if the whole lies just beyond the hill?

A townswoman said, *One day, the specialists will have put us all back together, and then they'll be gone.* The train was crowded with boys wearing their scars like medals, and each face as it turned to me said, I am part of an incident that will leave you forever piecing together details.

But the thoughts were eager to mount black beauties and canter straight into the trembling black burr of the storm. So seldom given their head, so rarely released to the attractor, and so knowing the furred curves of the favored path —

There would be penalties. As when the mind ventures beyond the fence plotted and built for its own good. Meanwhile the quarter-notes were piling up, all waiting for their proper placement on disinterested, unending staves.

In and Out of the Museum

Whither goest the treasurer? I saw the butterfly with its royal burden. I recognized something I can no longer explain.

Imagine portering your beauty in public, your maps unberibboned, all routes laid bare for any old wicked traveler

I had appointed a treasurer, but he stole all my gold. And then my head was turned by a random butterfly — I recognized something —

Flowering, flowering through the dusk. And on the outskirts: a quiet figure by the fence, swatting her bouquet of selves.

Do not ask about the silhouettes. There was darkness, and a bed, and a thief. There was a meadow bare of metaphor

Who but the butterfly could bear to lay all cards on the table: besotted after besotted besotted wing (so said the slow caterpillar)

Something about those unsnuffable torches, those sewn strangers (— I stood watching the treasurer cantering off with *my gold* down the dirt road —)

The butterfly was for rent. But only the metaphor-hunter was changing his spots, crying *Lepidoptera larder thief!*

So the monks were copying texts, so the butterflies were threading the torn stuff of the garden, so symbol and import met and desired to kiss.

But look a little closer at the butterfly: the tiny black burglar of the body, the deep arcadian loot of the stolen wings

That day in the museum — but let us not begin the reductivity. That day in the museum — but don't forget the butterfly was a sexual idea. That day in the museum — I recognized something I can no longer explain.

Guilty or Innocent

(1)

That a city park is not nature has its schools. I still remember the fog, how it rubbed thresholds to nothing. Gardenias eye us through balcony rails, caged birds — yet who is moved by this rather than the fatefulness of color

(2)

He said, "The city park is just a paperweight snowy with trained petals." He said, "A flower inside a vase can hardly call itself a flower."

(3)

From the window of the car the green meadows make me a promise they cannot keep. The eye is a better traveler than the foot, ravaging reverie with each step

(4)

"The city park," he said, "is about as 'natural' as the tigers yawning behind bars at the zoo." I sank to my knees and crushed a blade of grass in my hand — but this *is* dirt, and worms are stitching through the earth, and the planted flowers rotate helplessly to face the sun

(5)

At night the wife remembers the days before her husband, how the boys who gave her golden charms and called and called offered acres of virgin forest for the fairness of her hand

(6)

I remember he said: "The city park, in fact, is just another form of nostalgia — like a landscape painting"

(7)

the brown hills that never were wilderness bewitching, the oval lake that never said translucence inviting

(8)

In the epicenter of the untouched copse, a single gum wrapper glitters. In the shallows of 'I love you' swims a school of tiny gold doubts. The fog was darkening, the thresholds were tightening down.

The Fortune

It is a place for which some have spent their lives
sighing, a place of burnt-sugar plains and golden weight.
Note how the flowers are untroubled. Though secrets
are buried all around them in the dirt, their petals are
white and not off-white.

As to what is revealed — the sky with its great
loaves and fishes alludes a little. "To believe in happi-
ness," the fortune said, "is to worship at the altar of
unhappiness." Other sagesse waits, enthroned on your
shelves, with grand indifference for your hand.

When the flashlight has illuminated every hiding-
place in the house, the insomniac may sleep, dowsing
suspicions like sparks one by one. Then the camera
pans from the contented face of the sleeper to the ear-
ring lying at an unnatural angle on the stair.

What if you could set aside a bit of what might save you for when the coming abundance dies — oh, as it does — on the vine? Just a minute ago there were vistas, seascapes, bellevues, panoramas — now your one small room and its swags.

One summer I saw a girl sunbathing like a grave in a bed of obstreperous weeds. I have seen grown men and women nestle down into filthy sheets. The map was torn right where the little starred destination should have been.

The fortune said, "It's not that the world keeps secrets from you, but that you let yourself be crushed by its secrets." The policeman turned the corner. Some lighthouses are not benevolent, but halo each egress with incriminating white.

See sympathy, the tugboat? Its captain keeps no log for the notes of the beloved, who is plotting his own course all the while. And, incandescent with the light of their misapprehension, the lovers are tugged through the dark to open sea.

(1)

If gray clouds staining the night sky mean the firmament is in need of a cleaning, what does that say about the amour-propre of my mind? And if the iron wheels of the iron tram make a sound of guttural grief as they grind into meandering tracks,

(2)

I'm talking about nighttime. Too much has been made of the "corporality" of silence — if I can cut it with a knife, why can't I caress it. The guessed-at curve in the dark fathom of the bowl — and besides there is the clock ticking its teeth in the next room. Its face is choked with hour hands

(3)

The books lie gentle around my room like circumstantial leaves. In November, the leaves' ginger rust was seared in leaf-shapes onto sidewalks after rain. I followed the path once to see if the universe *does* beckon gingerly. Histrionics under the bridge require a river

(4)

The darkness is closing ranks. The first little staircase of notes floats tentatively through emptied streets. Certain kinds of glass shatter quietly. The morning-glory was tightening its frail Victrolas around the tender new shoot. I repeat myself: the tender new shoot. I repeat myself:

(5)

You can walk for miles before discovering what it was you really wanted to see. You can talk for hours before you realize you won't say it. When balconies all over this city come raining down around us, I will ask, Is surrender enough? And what I'm really asking of course is

(6)

It only dawned on me later, how at the magic show it was only the women's hands that shot up to be sliced in half. His lovely assistant shimmered: fruition. It's said the fox hunt is necessary to keep the fox alive, but days keep frothing up magically as the snowy fur of

(7)

It's not easy living next to a church in a medieval city. If you're suspicious often enough, now and then your suspicions will bear little glittering fruit. "The way to look at abstract paintings," a man told me once, "is to pretend you are lying down and looking up at the night sky." I was very young of course. Now no one can tell me how or where or when or who

(8)

The mist clouded the vista. . . . What was it I was not supposed to be seeing? I eyed every alley for egress, I beheld every portal for return. In this city as in any you can see the damnedest things. Each toll of the church bell striking nine was aimed at me, like an angel's finger damning me from within its frothy sleeve

(9)

If I want the evening locked up in a stone and held for dear life by the tiny silver claws of a mounting, who will disengage me? The restaurant opens. And at other times, in a landlocked place, I miss the sea so much I am the sailor in whose eyes the mistral churns. A forest of spires ought to be taken lying down

(10)

Equal parts desire and yoke. Equal parts gossamer and dirt. This evening the city is strung with girls held aloft on balconies like half-notes floating over the cages of their staves. And now I begin making my way, on foot, to the river

A Swan

Some nights aren't savable. Stars have their price. A boy buys a star-book with a certain girl in mind. If he connects the suspected dots, he wins a swan. There is no one to disagree, no one to inform him stars are only stars. Someone opens a book to a picture of a skeleton, sits down, and learns.

The boy is a little house still mostly dark with innocence. It is this opacity that is hard, for those who think they know what they are looking for. Light by light will come on until he is as visible as anyone in the room. He will find her secret star. The planetarium never asks permission.

The night sky comes into focus one star at a time. I learned the constellations and then forgot them, because a certain superfluity shone. I learned which flower is the cosmos-flower. I remembered the plots of books until they refused to stay constellated.

One room is lit up, and one is dark. Which room will the boy enter? In which room would he stay? The white horse looked beyond my sugar-cube from under its long lashes, the horse was a long-legged insect several hills away. A random arrangement of white horses marked the hillside.

Inside the body it's dark. But maybe the bones glow. The clasp broke on the girl's necklace of stars. There was no swan in the sky, and then there was. There was a white trumpeter swan in a picture book, and one night the boy distractedly locked its name into place.

The Contemporary Poetry Series

Edited by Paul Zimmer

The Contemporary Poetry Series

Edited by Bin Ramke

Arthur Vogelsang, *Twentieth Century Women*
Sidney Wade, *Empty Sleeves*
Liz Waldner, *Dark Would (The Missing Person)*
Marjorie Welish, *Casting Sequences*
Susan Wheeler, *Bag 'o' Diamonds*
C. D. Wright, *String Light*
Katayoon Zandvakili, *Deer Table Legs*
Andrew Zawacki, *By Reason of Breakings*

DATE DUE

			PRINTED IN U.S.A.